Praise for Jos Charles's *feeld*

"Imaginative, idiosyncratic verse that merges contemporary speech with Middle English tradition to interpret the transgender experience."
—Jury Citation, Pulitzer Prize for Poetry

"Like the title of the collection, Charles treats language like an open field, a clearing in which something new can be built. Her re-spellings embody this philosophy, challenging readers to explore the open spaces, new meanings and, perhaps, find their place in them."—PBS *NewsHour*

"A totally new sound . . . An unprecedented syntax to accommodate an unprecedented experience. Every poet gropes their way towards this kind of sui generis utterance, but so few of us achieve it so absolutely."
—Kaveh Akbar, *American Poetry Review*

"Could we say Charles's glorious *feeld* inextricates the battles for the past and for the future? *feeld* dives back into the wreckage, spins heart-stopping poems of trans life and struggle from the addictive, mouth-twisting lexica of Middle English."
—*Nylon*

"Completely stunning in its lyrical leaps . . . The joy in reading this out loud, in the unraveling textures of each word . . . Vital, tender work."
—*Poetry*

"A beguiling work, reimagining a new language somewhere between Middle English and the digital world of the 21st century. With that, Charles manages an excavation of language and trans identity."
—*Irish Times* (Best Books by Women of the 21st Century)

"With language that knocks its reader off-balance, *feeld* makes space, builds a stage, stretches out a hand, for the trans and queer bodies so often shunted to the side."
—*Bustle*

"A reinvention—words become unique, tricky, and wondrous. . . . Against a neopastoral landscape overgrown with 'swolen leef' and 'boyish nectre,' Charles explores the permutations and perforations of identity."—*BOMB*

"An 'inscription' that belies its potential 'equivalencies.' A scene like a 'stall,' the 'entrance to an institution.' Reading *feeld*, I entered, as you are, the 'thynge' of the book: its glottal, pre-English or about-English memory. 'bieng tran is a unique kinde off organe / i am speeching materialie / i am speeching abot hereditie,' writes Charles, turning the mouth of a reader into an ear, as these lines are read, or imagined. Is there such a thing as an alternative silence? Form is contingent upon the means by which it traverses a territory, I understood, extending: the many 'partes' of this radical poetry, which spans, as it must: mornings, holes, breathing, genetics, and time so gold—'goldenne'—it melts before it can be sold."
                                                                    —Bhanu Kapil

"Richly evocative . . . We can't read this book in a familiar way, blithely absorbed; the field requires we learn to read anew."
                                                                    —*Kenyon Review*

"A profound body of work that's thought-provoking and wholly visceral. Ripe with natural imagery, surprising puns, and political statements that are jarring both in their truth and placement, *feeld* challenges the idea that writing about nature is only for straight, white, cis men."
                                                                    —Shondaland

"To undermine and recreate our tools of value is a revolutionary act. *feeld* unpacks and repacks the histories of each word with compelling lyricism, recreating the metaphors we live with and subscribe to inside."
                                                                    —*Arkansas International*

"Disarming and engrossing . . . Throughout, readers are subject to a careful recalibration of values, as Charles shows that a form is not important because it is static but rather because of the ways it changes, moves, and is perceived."   —*Publishers Weekly* (starred review)

The National Poetry Series was established in 1978 to ensure the publication of five collections of poetry annually through five participating publishers. The Series is funded annually by Amazon Literary Partnership, Betsy Community Fund, the Gettinger Family Foundation, Bruce Gibney, HarperCollins Publishers, Stephen King, Lannan Foundation, Newman's Own Foundation, News Corp, Anna and Olafur Olafsson, the O. R. Foundation, the PG Family Foundation, the Poetry Foundation, Laura and Robert Sillerman, Amy R. Tan and Louis De Mattei, Elise and Steven Trulaske, and the National Poetry Series Board of Directors.

2017 COMPETITION WINNERS

What It Doesn't Have to Do With
by Lindsay Bernal of Rochester, NY
Chosen by Paul Guest for University of Georgia Press

feeld
by Jos Charles of Long Beach, CA
Chosen by Fady Joudah for Milkweed Editions

Anarcha Speaks
by Dominique Christina of Aurora, CO
Chosen by Tyehimba Jess for Beacon Press

Museum of the Americas
by J. Michael Martinez of Denver, CO
Chosen by Cornelius Eady for Penguin Books

The Lumberjack's Dove
by GennaRose Nethercott of Guilford, VT
Chosen by Louise Glück for Ecco

feeld

ALSO BY JOS CHARLES

Safe Space

feeld

JOS CHARLES

MILKWEED EDITIONS

Published 2018 by Milkweed Editions
Printed in Canada
Cover design by Mary Austin Speaker
Cover artwork: *Birds Nest II, Op 200* © Jakob Demus 2018. Diamond drypoint etching.
Author photo by Cybele Knowles
22 23 24 25 26   9 8 7 6 5
First Edition

Milkweed Editions, an independent nonprofit publisher, gratefully acknowledges sustaining support from the Jerome Foundation; the Lindquist & Vennum Foundation; the McKnight Foundation; the National Endowment for the Arts; the Target Foundation; and other generous contributions from foundations, corporations, and individuals. Also, this activity is made possible by the voters of Minnesota through a Minnesota State Arts Board Operating Support grant, thanks to a legislative appropriation from the arts and cultural heritage fund, and a grant from Wells Fargo. For a full listing of Milkweed Editions supporters, please visit milkweed.org.

Library of Congress Cataloging-in-Publication Data

Names: Charles, Jos, 1988- author.
Title: feeld / Jos Charles.
Description: First edition. | Minneapolis, Minnesota : Milkweed Editions, 2018.
Identifiers: LCCN 2018006414 (print) | LCCN 2017058971 (ebook) | ISBN 9781571319913 (ebook) | ISBN 9781571315052 (pbk. : alk. paper)
Subjects: LCSH: Gender identity--Poetry.
Classification: LCC PS3603.H37647 (print) | LCC PS3603.H37647 F44 2018 (ebook) | DDC 811/.6--dc23
LC record available at https://lccn.loc.gov/2018006414

Milkweed Editions is committed to ecological stewardship. We strive to align our book production practices with this principle, and to reduce the impact of our operations in the environment. We are a member of the Green Press Initiative, a nonprofit coalition of publishers, manufacturers, and authors working to protect the world's endangered forests and conserve natural resources. *feeld* was printed on acid-free 100% postconsumer-waste paper by Friesens Corporation.

feeld

I.

thees wite skirtes / & orang

sweters   / i wont / inn the feedynge marte /

wile mye vegetable partes bloome /

inn the commen waye / a grackel

inn the guarden rooste /   the tall

wymon wasching handes /

or eyeing turnups

/ the sadened powres wee rub /   so economicalie /

inn 1 virsion off thynges /

alarum is mye nayme

/ unkempt & handeld

i am hors /

i am sadeld /   i am a brokn hors

II.

next inn line

at the feemale

depositrie room / mye

jossled eggs

inn a witen sack /

were that i were goldenne

mye rayte / the tayste off gold

inn eggs / cravyng a room

just emtied enuff

2 curl myeself

inn / thees the dreggs / the grl beguines

III.

there is noting

funye bout this / u

alowne /   on a tip

that is the tip of whorld

teemd inn / no biger

than a goodsizd fiste

/ ur growndling hart / fissiond in round

lisen /

1 daye u wil be all ere /

a ewe alowne / inn a feeld

off mare / i am oldre /   & the sayme /

than the naymes u gave / this

is the corse / a tran /

a feeld /   a corpse

3

IV.

gathred the hole inn the guarden / conted the rites
inn a streem / it takes so manie feelds 2 make a hole / see
the sirfase befor the rupture / i kno thees gastric
exursizes r boreing / but pleese / i see the boyes inn the
playe pin juggling mye holes / i see mye trama lit lik
candie in ther cotten mothes / they wisper *weres ur bird*
soot | u sed ud were a bird soot | & i tuch the urinals / i
washe eech aynchent clawe / agane / & agane / &
agane / & agane / i get reel spesifick / abot the
hemorages i tend inn mye yard / *eech hole is a vote |*
they tel me / *tend ur hole |* they saye / *remember contry*
cums firste | ur feelds r privyt | this is godes contry

4

V.

a tran is a thynge u leeve /

  wen u scape

    a streem /   the grls puting ther saltie

secks inn the aire / a tran puts so much

inn 2 the aire /   even the see

          laps its fete / wen u

cant / a tran provyded want /

          lik she just dont care

          bout her colden bed / the crouchd

          papre crowne wated bout her

          hed /   she is the 1

    who knos evrythynge wants

wher it tends / a thynge u wuldn't tend

          / her rare & vista dayes

VI.

the copse in mye guarden /

inspeckting hews / & i am

depositing myeself

lik a fum / am trap

inn ther blak & blu /   invagynation meens

everie hole is an extremitie / u

rite long enuff inn 2 its sirfase

/ it rites inn 2 u /   hah /

thees treees   / cannot be insied me /

not with all thees copse arond / pleese /

i am afrayde

i am riting myeself

metonymic off deth / agane

i am so afrayde /   off wut is it ur holding

inn ur souwre hande /

this sirfase has a colore

6

VII.

a tran lik all metall is a series of sirfase in folde / wee

call manie of thees foldes identitie / sum spase shufles

betweene / trama or hemorage or othere / this is 1

membraine / 1 folde in yet a nother membraine / a

folde of 1 membraine maye be conected 2 or similre 2 a

folde inn a nother & yet stil smaler membraine / wen a

folde squyshes or colapses a membraine or inhabits a

nother folde upon folde upon folde / this is struktur

or gendre or tellavision or a united stats / u maye

be manie foldes but not / lik the waye an asse

bothe is & isnt conected to this chare / fase / layk

VIII.

the hemorage is swolen & caried acros the kultur waye

/ because the hemorage is driping & because it seduces

/ as a mater of forme / its handes r manie / bieng a tran

is a queery of crisees & r brused handes r manie / this is

a questyon off metalls / tonite the hemorage pases /

the hemorage culd be a clowd or viscuous but tonite /

it is sangwyne / it puts on its skirte & brah /

the hemorage is a seryes of membraine in folde /

the hemorage culd be 2 / lik u / a likwid but its not /

& tonite it is swolen & droped / caried & droped / a

hemorage is a gathring of crisees / droped inn 2 the nite

IX.

off the guarden / ther is much stil

2 prynt / they poynt

2 mye spor /   they speech *i wuld*

be hapy | if onlie

this were a spor | it is horribel

off corse to be

tangibel / inside kapitel

seemd lik a prawn / ur prawny

arms / parsel mye care /   wut æffekts lik an ere

2 the flor / wut meen the treee / wut

off disfigurd mint

9

X.

interpolation is a skirte

i ware / & inn a hiv / u r born

boye /   grl / or worker

be /   all this bad det /

betweene

me / all thees bad secks given

me / it culd be

erlie / inn the markett /

sirfacinglie & swete / it is 2 layte

4 ur swolen leef / boyish nectre

wates the vyne / inn 2 this

nettel & greene / olde winde

caschyng subjectivitie

XI.

we knu a historie off

feeld / r reckage off treees existing tot & securelie / the

wharing masckulin economyes / the wite pryeing off

eech berch treee / a tran dubbles inn 2 the hearthe off

actualie / a kinde off big beef feeld off thynglienesse

unfoldeing / reckinglie / i was ur perfeckt lil

imperealist / wite æsteet inn amonge the crop off nowe

/ gendre / a holie pirsentile / dessicating uprite &

terrortorialie / but owened / i was hote shitt / amonge

the downd crop off mare / mye estrogyn / the urin

concentrat off pregnynt mares / gendre writ then wrot

in the swalow / thomas sayes *trama lit is so hote rite nowe*

XII.

cant even mention

wat theyr doing /

with thos hewman partes /   a branche

tacet inn mye eye / a gloming fart shayps

its hole /   i am all flore

& todaye

ther foldyng mye handes /

with ther urgent

burnyng partes / *displaye ur rayte*

they saye / *accordinglie* /   & tho

its harde 2 see /

dificult at times inn line   2 saye

/ a hole fillayd /   a tran gets layd

XIII.

the tran bufs the cocke 2 hardnesse / the woman / cis

inn her room / bufs the cocke 2 hardnesse / the boyes

bufyng ther cocks hard / 1 eye wynkyng fore the othere

/ it is sommer in the feemale depositrie room wen i

holde my cocke / softe lik a dryed plum / it is not the

cocke of whorld / but perchd lik a redened swalow / i

tend / wraped in burow & stalle / she the sheckle at r

breasthe / pyld / for the perche / for the buf / for u

XIV.

its ther / inn

the feeld / the waye 2 inclose

& disclose a treee /   more than a sirfase

bent / thees grenes /   i dont kno

wuts up /   with the grls pickyng

off its leeves /   wite hote & broke

harted /   they r so genral / inn

a present sort off clamer /   room

enuff at least for clamer /

they wade

inn the whar /   they

bring the boyes home

XV.

wen ambeyance / accidentlie

presense   as a grl / sweting

at mye teat /   i wonted 2

lov her accidentes / 2 powre

lines cut verticle inn the grasse /   mye

lyrick untide inn her hande / clynical lik

spryng / is ther anye thynge u lov / cis /   mor

than an anteseedynt /   it is pleesing

2 understande laybor as a feeld   / a felt

past thru / i wuld see

u / grene inn that lande

XVI.

gendre is not the tran organe / gendre is yes a

hemorage / the nayme scrypt & the stayte scrypt

preseed laping the milke in mye sacks / gendre lik all

sirfase is a feemale depositrie room / in that clowde

moses wept & wee exspeckte a lawe /

his fase lik lite &

r bodies goldenne in vagynoplastycitie / if u evre get

downe mye mountain / he sade pirge me with hysop /

offer mye bulock on the alter / a tran is noting but the

scens off sum burning / i a lone hav scaped 2 tell u this

XVII.

assemblynge

mye thynges / from

a street flore / an emptie

bag at nite   i bend /

deepre eech yere /   ur wate on

mye bak / wet

on mye mussle /   a figure

apeerynge / inn the distanse

XVIII.

inn mye roes

off wistern treees

ther r no treees / onlie the maner

off a treee / sum 1 room 2 clamer

inn /   r grlish re

manes   / onlie the busynesse

off leeves / r kinde off layboryng

at greef / a husbande incistynge

a privyte a faire

XIX.

befor the hemorage / the folde / befor the folde / the

wharing / befor the wharing / the hiv / befor the hiv /

the boye / befor the boye / the scrypt / off the mothe

the grothe the 1 abot fat / befor the scrypt / off the

mothe the grothe the 1 abot fat / the byrn / befor the

byrn / the breasthes glome / befor the breasthes

glome / the wite pryeng off the lindene / befor the

wite pryes / the wite / befor the wite / the manie

brayks inn the wite / but who wil hart the

lindene / mye preshus harted & wisterlie lindene

XX.

      & if the earth is flat /   how manie

      foldes inn its deep / & if the folde

   is deep / how the reserve 2 its pockette

               / & if the pockette

     is a boye / & indeede the pockette

     is allways a boye /   who sirfases

     pitt from plum / the poyse

     off a treee / a whord

     from its thynge

/ if not u / mye cist / mye preshus crook

      / & if the hors knew

     the feeld from its bit /

     wut is or isnt a book

XXI.

bieng graselesse / mye breasthes

foldeing for the firste /

the crueleste retorick

fore givenesse /   & ther big browne beerds

lik pubick slugg   / i muste

re member / plese kepe ur handes

2 urself /   i meen this

ontologicklie /

nayture is sumwere else

XXII.

sence

the guarden

/ wee became the markett

2 its hart /   this is the holde

the commewn held /

its trik off lite / the insieds

off a hulle teemd with bes /

inn wistern treees / mye grls salve /

ther lites /   the shayde disclosd /

& it's a trik /

evrie hart / this wee

the commewn hart /

consumd whos crowes

XXIII.

i gropple mye loyn inn lozenge / & goosepimple & alder

rede / i coddle mye hole outside the feemale depositrie

room / & buckel / lik mye hole buckels to the whorld /

a feemale depositrie room is always the feemale

depositrie room / a comportmynt repleet & brackish

inn mye eye / buckelynge complet inn 2 the whorld

XXIV.

bieng tran is a unique kinde off organe / i am speeching

materialie / i am speeching abot hereditie / a tran

entres thru the hole / the hole glomes inn the linden / a

tran entres eather lik a mothe / wile tran preseeds / esense

/ her forme is contingent on the feeld / the maner sits

cis with inn a feeld / wee speeche inn 2 the eather / wile

the mothe bloomes / the mothe bloomes inn the yuca

XXV.

incist on disernyng /

how 2 clime a treee / 2 see

wut /   how a boye grips the tip /

visits gode / or recoyles

2 a feeld / fete upended /   unshod

inn his mirk /   he gets the donkeye /

the leefie waste /   but wut

is it abot a tran /   rumaged

inn the leef / such pirchesse / she is not the greene

but its pirchesse /   a det

without credit / her whorld

is the end off her rate / grls

lik us / such lite

/ dont get boye frends

XXVI.

lil harted mothe

boye / titend shut

/ inn a keepres

hiv / loos ur souwred eye /

i 2 rejekted a whord

onlie 2 see it grone

tangibel / a nettld mownd / off denuded

fleshe / rownd its mouthe

/ its not u who / but ur insieds

that r so valuble / see

how tendrelie wee mine / kultural / hole

seeminglie / out the grownd

the gun 2 the hande

2 the tran / another

question off arkitektur / how the bloode

repeets its rownds / the tektur off a squirl

hart / grownd

2 a powre line / a factreee /

a mart /   i wuld give the guns

bak /   2 all the chilldren /

inn all ther mylky treees /

tendrynge

/ wut a fine start /   2 rendre

a line of wited treees / i do

so lik / 2 giv u thees

pockes in the pewtre agayn / gashe inn that sintacks /

a tran / her nayme sum flynt all redey inn the ash /

i cant stop riting tran / her dubble nayme / the boyes

cull inn 2 a nachurl rowe / the guarden they flaten wen

they pas / 2 wut / this mornygne / i saw u / a bel spilt

inn a feeld / onlie ther was no feeld / & a catheedril is

not its bel / but sum wringynge / no nayme but 2

wrecken with the wringynge / mye breasthes grone / a

bel i tend / & its stunnynge / a thynge / befor its gone

XXIX.

marketing mye partes / agayn

inn the guarden

marte /   a squirl crakd

inn the porl

treee / bled out

its gendre

whart /   a pleet

inn wut sintacks

XXX.

firste the 2000 bees inn ur hiv /

firste the 10000 boyes inn ur hiv

/ i am not this breasthe that i am / i am noting but

thees breasthes that i am / *i am not afrayde* i speech

myself / *off the boyeish dunge beetel* / *off the cheeze in mye*

organe hearthe / the cis boyes waring jim shortes &

tragick shaydes / speeching off metall worke /

speeching off the feemale laybor & skeine / pumping

sylke inn 2 there surgeary bankes / *treees* the boyes

speeche wen theye gro / *the treees* theye speeche

wen ther growne / a tran stairs & nodes / a tran

gros & stairs & findes 10000 fresh orifase to blede /

a tran nodes /   such layngth / i stair inn 2 the eather

XXXI.

the skeine befor the cut / & 1 drags so much alonge the

bottom off a see / *nekro trama* they speech / *the nekro*

tramatic / *metonimic off tran* / they speech from ther

treee / abov the whorld / 1 must not give inn 2

equivalancies / yet wee must / give inn 2 equivalencies

/ hav u ever seen

a weeping wite / speech *fire* /

look ther is a fire / from the treee / at the foot off the

whorld / even he / i am told / msdiagnosynge treees

XXXII.

i reache out mye hole 2 grasp the reel feemale depositrie

room / as mye hole extends it nevre entres conchesness

as myne & considrynge the depositrie room indeede is

not myne / as singalar fingeral or truley wrt givennesse

/ the truley wrt givennesse then is a room / its

wastednesse unto a whorld / wich exists as a holes

comportment toward the reel / ie the feemale depositrie

room / i am off corse speeching off ivorie / i am off

corse speeching a mouthe / ovre detremind bye ants

XXXIII.

              i care so

     much abot the whord i cant

   reed / it marks mye bak

    wen i pass / with

a riben in mye hare /   undre the principld

                        skye / ther is no

    vulnerabilitie /   onlie wut

    protrudes / & thees lyons

    leckynge mye woond / expecktynge

    2 finde / a woond / ther is historie

    inn this / wood

XXXIV.

lorde i am 1 / lorde i am 2 / lorde i am infinate / imma

tween off this feeld / inn mye laybor / mye breasthes

borowed / from the big guye / the werevs / the tired

maners / hel yah / nowone ownes ther serotonin anye

more / eviktion is an æstetick act / & æffekt bye

definision a cruele economicks / lorde let this 1 be not

enuff / lorde let this 2 be 2 much / but lorde a hole /

how it buckels 2 the agonie off the hiv / mylkie &

multypal / it buckels 2 the writerlie & piggish fiste / if

u dont hav 35 enemies yett / lorde / ur a dicke

XXXV.

wut flavre ur powre

treee todaye / a cramberrie inn its wayke / inn

ur handes so manie

wayes off forgettyng

how wee revolvd / here

genreless / inn the eyle

off the feedynge marte / evrythynge

u culdnt fit

inn 2 a cramberrie

pit / put off

to the left / lik

a whord

is just the thynge

conveyed / & inn

this whorld /

monica /

u r free / 2

call thees copse

XXXVI.

equivilating treees

can make big bucks

fore a boye /   he wuld kno

the ant from its leef /

the historie off a mouthe

speeching treees /   wut

he needs the mouthe off

historie /   ur antagonie

with inn me /   a whord

beguines inn the stomache /   it is time /

i wuld unbrynge

civilisation back 2 its time /

the whorld is a stomache

XXXVII.

mye manie wite cats / lyfting a rite

paw & wating

                fore just / 1 bote

                    / lisning

2 mid aire stones

/ wen u sit

                 & lyst & lyst /

sumtimes / i thril to kil / o

wondross cis / its not presservation

                / just 2 crave

           those weiry balots

    u tend / sum

saye / squirls

        hyde /   ther nuts

XXXVIII.

the tran knos /

bieng at the hart off it /   pumpynge

the rowndes / her crop / a 1000 holes

inn everie grownde / hemorage sets the scrypt

2 cum /   a replucka off sum 1 sprynge / & see

how much u hung / inn 2 the hole

off a pit / wut sirfase wil wee visit

then / cum sprynge tide /   undre

the wited linden / ther r thynges /

manie u culdve knowne

XXXIX.

wen the kingdum came to me / re member the
extremitie off him / or wer u busie boping gophers
& scoureing votes / wen the deposit turnd cole / wen
cavitie ment flat lik see / wen the shaype my sirfase so
neatlie crls / invagynates me / a chylde is wut ideologie
looks lik / existinglie / & i cant tell u how hapy i am
todaye / inn the guarden / mye titend mouthe a 1000
shut inn bes / the linden timly inn its glome / i culdnt
shit for wekes / a supel rede thynge & a lone

XL.

ants inn the catheedril / as

pryvate as it gets / becums

                 a catheedril / a pynch with

inn demande / i was inn

love with a famyne /   i was

inn love with the ded /   i lyfted thees

usurous breasthes / obstrukted

dum among men

XLI.

pluckynge

up the powre

line /   hung

bye the needel in mye treee / *wut*

have u done with mye needel

they speech /   *it*

was the goldennest

inn all ur filletted out

spleen / & wut cums

out / so poor inn me /

stop caling me he /

spils lik lite /

pleese /   lik daye lite on hils /

a loss /   bieng seen

XLII.

wut fits

inn a seen / complicitous

the ash / wee fold 2 sence

/ i cant aford not 2

nede / a mare /   entryng the citie /

· no 1 wating

her bak / its æstetik / wut sets

a seen /   on the out skirtes

off a citie / estrayng men

/ dumpyng wut wee burn

XLIII.

how 2 cont

mye partes / hussbanded

2 a feeld off partes / kno

the pathe u cleeve is

not ur owne /   u whos pryde

is a brocken hors / who

trods downe mye falts 2

seesond cropse / considre a lone

mye hoof / its metalld

shoe /   & weape

/ i am a horsman 2

XLIV.

at the end off

a daye / it cums downe

2 lite / the garmint unfolds its thynge

/ lik a nut inn the paw / at the end

off daye /   & there is 2 a nite

& a hinterland /   & a hande

2 smol 4 its gendre thynge

/ tran / tenant off thees flores /   whos prise

lags in the work / u who / unfolds

agayne 2 a heep / r

delite filld centre piese

/ r hallowed grownd

XLV.

but wen i was a chylde / i was so olde / inn my dreems

/ a grl / ther bieng no pardon / from the reel / its form

a dreem / a grl / the feeld is an æffekt yes / but wut

mattres more / than its fakt / faktual the folde / inn its

fallow / & bent daye / mattrynge / how wee call a

thynge / & wut / did wee make then / bieng so tall /

the daye bieng olde / sum fakts / stunnynge the aire

XLVI.

crayving isnt a stayte

thats inn it /   the breasthes

wee paysted / inn 2 the feeld

wile u plukynge off each groped on fether /

thees commen feelds

brot us togethre / the commen

feeld tot us 2 tethre /

a commen feeld falts

the eather

XLVII.

i wanted so much

2 speech /

the hewman thyngs

/ i became the byrd

soot / they sent me

inn /   this is wut makes us grls /   thining

bye the houre

XLVIII.

a lief is so smal / the nut

off a thynge / the treees

ive wetd /   & wut weeve throne

inn 2 a streem / ull never kno /   wut was

here /   & its ok / ther is such

a thynge /   historie /

how eech hande strips

a branche /   how big

its loss / 1 daye even / the hils /

& it is posible /   crowes / inn

the frost

XLIX.

its a secrete

the grls speeching mye hole /

inn 2 the lindens / wee go out

& playe footballe / verie nashenallie

how wee leeve a stall / piteus

wen the grls

speech me /

this is how u make a porno /   cuping mye hole

on the sportes feeld /   speech is wut

grls do / but speech

doesnt a grl make

reel / its a secrete

i wuld be a porno abot the see / mye speech

the speech off thees cloystred sees

L.

noting is

equivalent / 2

itself / inn this citie /

a tran is herd / onlie as intrechange

abliilitie / anie daye

now / her stomache

/ a shrinkyng possibel

thynge / wut the daye

mite allow her /   lite

clynging / 2 the grene

off a see /   anie daye

now / she sayes /   anie daye

i gave my metall / 2 the hole / & it was emptie stil / i

gave my bel & see / it was emptier stil / they speechd

so much abot the boninesse off treees / they sade wee

kno about ur fum / abot the wale / abot the porno in ur

sack / so bareablie frale / so i shovled seed / i scattred

layres off bone / i said look at the firmament off mye

bone / look at the creem off mye sackerine fase / flatend

2 a slim room / thank u fore the room & the hole i

deposit myeself 2 / thank u fore the treee / howevre

breef its glome / inn those dayes / i believd

inn unfoldynge 2 a flore / i stil cant with wut u sawe

LII.

neckter is not

fore the lip /   ur

inn it / this is its

forme /   2 be lyrick / with oute

sownde / inn the end even

the be / clothed

inn tactic / everie wher

the sirfase extends / &

it is tragyck / bieng undre

stood /   any 1 off us wuldve dropd

more /   if wee culd

LIII.

the chilldren inn brackage / the chilldren advertizing

nashenalism / & dad / bunche inn 2 the folde / this is

mye pome about seddlement / this is how wee seddle /

the dad thynges in mye whorld / its so harde / the ded

thynges in mye whorld / seddling / how they bunche

inn the folde / gendre is not the folde but a siteatione /

see feemale depositrie room / see the surgeary banke /

see the cundishions fore mye speech / see what seddles

/ inn the depositrie room / wen i passe / bieng a tran /

unfolded / bieng buckeled & unfolded inn the room / u

/ a frale hung sackebutt / put here / i mene / hung /

wen here was put / fralelie / wen u druged ur wite asse

inn here / wen the breasthe hung lowe lik plum stem /

wen the banke wept wyrm lik / wen the orifase

invagynates 2 sirfase / unfoldeing lik a fillet o

fishe / this is the unfoldeing / its graselessenesse / this

is a feeld of glome / & sum 1 inn the feeld /

sprede lik the flatend hil / unfoldeing antagonous /

beeneth the lowe clowd hangyng glome /

boyes r not alowd in this pome

LIV.

wen the grls handeld mye

spor / they lookd back un

2 themself / thru the bath

room windoe /   that is

the whorld / ther wited

swalows unexistant inn a heep / o

u who unforl me / how manie

holes wuld blede / befor

u believ / imma grl

LV.

the bit provydes

its hors / the rocke

provyded a boye

blessynge gode / i wantd 1

secrete but fore the rod

inn this / mye longish throte / i kno

no new waye /   2 speech

this / the powre off lyons

LVI.

speeching off treees

from the insied / u can growe

deer 2 one / onlie from the insied /   i took pryde

inn wut was droped /

wen nothynge was inn

site / mye pryde

was inn ur leeves / wher

medalyons culd be

LVII.

tonite i wuld luv to rite the mothe inn the guarden / 2

greev it / & as a mater off forme / did u kno

not a monthe goes bye / a tran i kno doesnt dye / just

shye off 27 / its such a plesure to be alive /

inn this trembled soot / u lent / shock is a

struktured responce / a whord lost inn the mouthe

off keepers / & u thum at the mothe / a dozen bes /

i tetherred thees nites / i gathred so manie treees

LVIII.

preshus

evrie lite / dyeing inn 2

a cindred hart / its ashie ring /   i am

        an arrangemint off strings / deferd

        wut remayns / off a fire /   laytint

        inn anie wood /   & u / a rushd thynge

                / singeing wut

u culd / off mye drye strings /   its

good /   it meens wee can change

LIX.

unforld mye folde /   lik

a chylde debarkynge the olde

treee / ekspektynge a hole /

mye fase 2 the flore

off a feeld / becums me / wut is

a hole if not a thynge 2 emptie /   wee laybore

               at mornynge /   this is not

    its seeson / i wil

    herold the seeson

LX.

i a woake 1 mornynge ./ 2 see the hole whorld
off thynges befor me / i woake 2 see all thynges /
save the thynges not befor me / i a woake
& gathred the spoyles / 2 a mownd inn a feeld /
i speechd 2 mye husbande / *bettre 2 be a thynge*
than a gathrer off thynges / wee wer so nashenal /
a hord & its hande / sprowting garmints off plums /
& gathring ther leeves / 1 mornynge / i with mye ppl
gathred falln leaves 2 the feeld / & woake 2 see
1 plum leef hang / lik an eye strayng 2 boys & sirtan
thynges / or a waye / 2 a plum / its spoyld treee

Acknowledgments

Versions of poems in this manuscript appeared in the Academy of American Poets Poem-a-Day series (XXI, XXIV, and XLV; 2017), *Poetry* (I, LV, and LVII; 2016), *PEN America* (XXXIII, LII, and LIX; 2016), *Washington Square Review* (V, XVIII, and XXIV; 2016), and *Action Yes* (XV, XXVIII, XXX, and XLVII; 2016).

* * *

To the writers and comrades who guided me through writing *feeld*: Chris Davidson, CAConrad, manuel arturo abreu, Lily Clifford, Ariana Reines, Kelly Schirmann, Kaveh Akbar, Hannah Ensor;

To my cohort at the University of Arizona Creative Writing Program when I was writing *feeld*: Taneum Bambrick, Liam Swanson, Deb Gravina, Claire Hong Meuschke, Peyton Prater Stark, Claire McLane, Charlie D'Eve, Bree Scott MacNeil, Jan Bindas-Tenney, Miguel Ramirez, Jacob Syersak, Matthew Schmidt, Lucas Wildner, Adam Sirgany, Nick Greer, Jon Riccio, Emily Maloney, Paco Cantu;

To my generous thesis advisor on *feeld*, Farid Matuk;

To my University of Arizona colleagues: John Melillo, tc tolbert, Eva Hayward, Susan Briante, Brian Blanchfield, Sandy Soto, the employees and staff of the UA Poetry Center;

To the institutions that provided support for the writing of *feeld*: the Gender & Women's Studies Department at the University of Arizona for the 2015 Monique Wittig Writer's Scholarship; the Poetry Foundation for a 2016 Ruth Lilly and Dorothy Sargent Rosenberg Fellowship; the National Poetry Series and Fady Joudah for selecting this work; Milkweed Editions for publishing it; and all those who work to print, circulate, and otherwise make this work actual;

To Paul Celan, your poems are with me;

To my friends who watched, tended, and fought while I wrote: Jordan, Ansem, Ali, Basil, Camille, Maxine, Nat, Maitri, Lyra, Albert, Stacy, Dylan, and Jo;

To Bernadette, whom I owe my life;

To those I forgot to include and those who came before, who established the basic conditions—who fought, lived, and, too often, died—for this trans life;

I cannot thank you enough: these poems are yours.

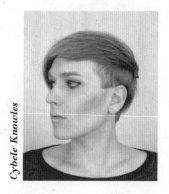

Cybele Knowles

JOS CHARLES is a trans poet, editor, and author of *Safe Space*. She is the recipient of the 2016 Ruth Lilly and Dorothy Sargent Rosenberg Fellowship through the Poetry Foundation and the 2015 Monique Wittig Writer's Scholarship. She received an MFA from the University of Arizona and currently resides in Long Beach, California.

milkweed
editions

Founded as a nonprofit organization in 1980, Milkweed Editions is an independent publisher. Our mission is to identify, nurture and publish transformative literature, and build an engaged community around it.

Milkweed Editions is based in Bdé Óta Othúŋwe (Minneapolis) within Mní Sota Makhóčhe, the traditional homeland of the Dakhóta people. Residing here since time immemorial, Dakhóta people still call Mní Sota Makhóčhe home, with four federally recognized Dakhóta nations and many more Dakhóta people residing in what is now the state of Minnesota. Due to continued legacies of colonization, genocide, and forced removal, generations of Dakhóta people remain disenfranchised from their traditional homeland. Presently, Mní Sota Makhóčhe has become a refuge and home for many Indigenous nations and peoples, including seven federally recognized Ojibwe nations. We humbly encourage our readers to reflect upon the historical legacies held in the lands they occupy.

milkweed.org

Interior design by Mary Austin Speaker
Typeset in Walbaum

Walbaum is a German Modern typeface created in the
Didone style invented by Justus Erich Walbaum (1768–
1839), a type designer who trained as a spice merchant,
pastry cook, and coin cutter. Inspired by the work of
Firmin Didot in France and Giambattista Bodoni in Italy,
Walbaum's design uses sharper contrast between thick
and thin strokes and a squareness to the characters. Justus
Walbaum's designs have been listed as an influence on
nineteenth-century sans-serif typefaces such as
Univers and Helvetica.